This one is for my youngest nephews back east:
The Butler boys — Isaac and Elliot.
And the Squires boys — Jake and Jonah.
T. F.

And for my nephew, Ozzie.
T. E.

First published in 2024 by Nosy Crow Ltd.
in collaboration with the British Museum.
Wheat Wharf, 27a Shad Thames
London, SE1 2XZ, UK

This edition published 2025 by Nosy Crow Inc.
145 Lincoln Road
Lincoln, MA 01773, USA

ISBN 979-8-88777-154-0

Nosy Crow and associated logos are trademarks
and/or registered trademarks of Nosy Crow Ltd.
Used under license.

Text by Tegen Evans
Text © 2024 by Nosy Crow
Illustrations © 2024 by Tom Froese

Library of Congress Catalog Card Number 2024945403.

All rights reserved.

No part of this publication may be reproduced, stored in a retrieval system, or transmitted
in any form or by any means (electronic, mechanical, photocopying, recording, or otherwise)
without the prior written permission of Nosy Crow Ltd.

The publisher and copyright holder prohibit the use of either text or illustrations to develop any generative
machine learning, artificial intelligence (AI) models, or related technologies.

Printed in Dongguan, China, following rigorous ethical sourcing standards.

1 3 5 7 9 10 8 6 4 2

Roman Soldiers Contents

What was a Roman soldier?	Page 4
How was the Roman army organized?	Page 6
What uniform and weapons did soldiers need?	Page 8
How did soldiers train?	Page 10
How did soldiers fight in battle?	Page 12
What did cavalry soldiers do?	Page 14
What was a siege?	Page 16
What happened if soldiers were injured?	Page 18
What was life like in the forts?	Page 20
Where did soldiers live when they were on the move?	Page 22
What happened when the army won a battle?	Page 24
Glossary	Page 26
Index	Page 27

What was a Roman soldier?

Over 2,000 years ago, the ancient city of Rome invaded many countries, creating the powerful Roman Empire. It was one of the largest empires to have ever existed, with an amazing army of soldiers. The Roman army became famous throughout the ancient world for its clever tactics, impressive organization, and success in battle.

Only men could join the Roman army. Half of the soldiers in the Roman army were called "legionaries." They had to be citizens of the Roman Empire. Most people from the many countries around the world that were ruled by Rome were not citizens but could still join the army as "auxiliaries." They were usually paid less than legionaries and their work was sometimes more dangerous.

It wasn't easy to become a Roman soldier. You had to be in shape and very strong, have good eyesight, and be over five feet and five inches tall. It was helpful if you knew how to read or write (most people then could not), and any hopeful soldier had to ask someone important to write a letter recommending them. You could join the army when you were a teenager, but whatever age you were, you had to be prepared to spend the next 25 years of your life in the army!

Life was very tough for Roman soldiers. They were treated harshly, faced great danger, and the training was exhausting. But they were also paid pretty well, and they had food to eat and somewhere to sleep. If a legionary survived for the full 25 years, they would be rewarded with land or money which they could use to build a home and start a farm. An auxiliary soldier would be rewarded by being made a Roman citizen.

How was the Roman army organized?

The Roman army was organized into lots of small groups, or units.

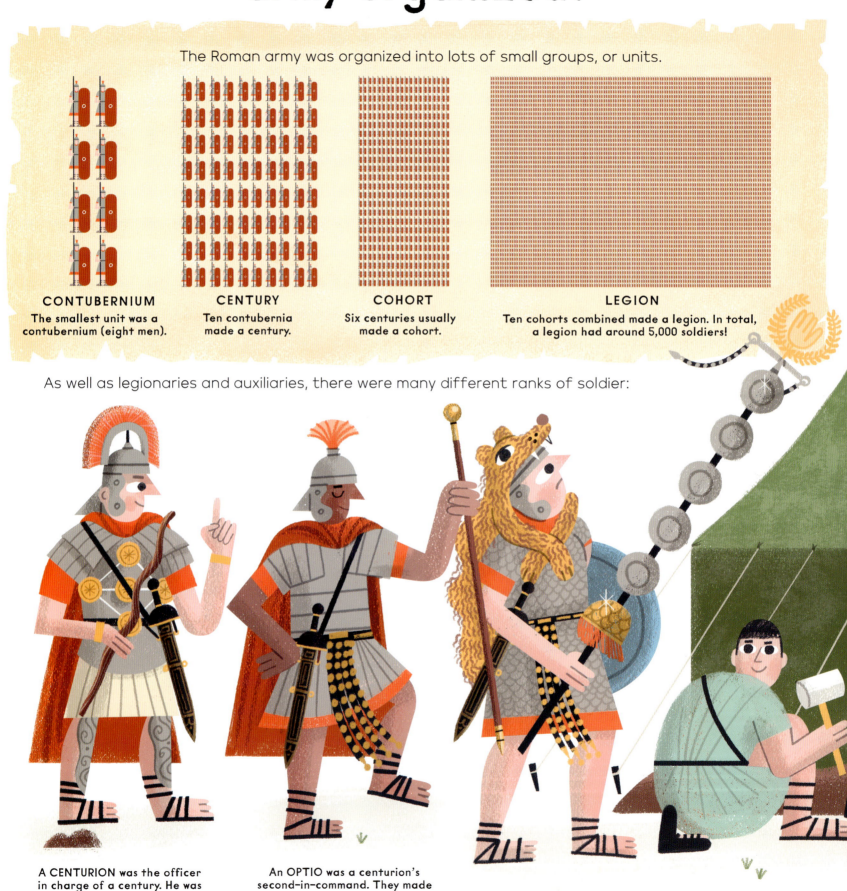

CONTUBERNIUM
The smallest unit was a contubernium (eight men).

CENTURY
Ten contubernia made a century.

COHORT
Six centuries usually made a cohort.

LEGION
Ten cohorts combined made a legion. In total, a legion had around 5,000 soldiers!

As well as legionaries and auxiliaries, there were many different ranks of soldier:

A CENTURION was the officer in charge of a century. He was brave, tough, and carried a wooden rod to beat soldiers with if they didn't work hard enough!

An OPTIO was a centurion's second-in-command. They made sure that everyone stayed in line and kept up during marches.

A STANDARD BEARER assisted a centurion and calculated soldiers' pay. In battle they stood in front of the soldiers, carrying a large pole with a badge or flag on it.

A PRAEFECTUS CASTRORUM was a senior soldier in charge of the fort or camp when the army was on the move.

The EMPEROR was the person in charge of the Roman Empire. They were also the commander-in-chief of the Roman army. He encouraged the soldiers to fight in battle and made sure they were paid regularly.

TRIBUNES worked closely with the legate and learned from him for when their time came to become a legate.

A LEGATE commanded the entire legion. He had to be a senator (a rich politician) and was chosen by the emperor himself.

What uniform and weapons did soldiers need?

A Roman soldier had to buy his own uniform and weapons, and spent a lot of time cleaning and polishing his armor—rust had to be avoided at all costs.

A heavy metal HELMET protected a soldier's head, ears, and neck. Soldiers attached dyed horsehair crests to the top of their helmets so that they looked taller and so officers could be quickly identified by the rest of the army.

Underneath their armor, soldiers wore a linen or woolen TUNIC, which was a bit like a short dress, held up with a belt.

A MANICA (armored sleeve) could be worn to protect the sword arm.

On their legs, soldiers could wear pants called BRACAE. Some soldiers also wore metal leg guards (GREAVES), too.

For battle, metal armor was worn over the tunic. Some soldiers wore a heavy CHAIN MAIL VEST, made of metal rings linked together.

Others wore a METAL CUIRASS, which was a breastplate and backplate made of flexible sections. These gave better protection but were so heavy that soldiers had to help each other put them on.

How did soldiers train?

Every day, Roman soldiers had to spend many tough hours in training. This involved marching, practice-fighting, handling weapons, and obeying trumpet signals. Soldiers had to be as skilled and in shape as possible because they could be needed for battle at any moment.

The most common drill was the route march, a 20-Roman-mile march (which is about 18 modern miles) that had to be completed in five hours. Soldiers had to keep step in time with one another while carrying weapons, a shield, food rations, cooking equipment, and a spade. The total weight of each soldier's kit was about the same as carrying a nine-year-old child!

Soldier Slip-Ups!
When soldiers asked the emperor Vespasian for more "shoe money" because they were marching so much that their sandals were wearing out, Vespasian responded by making the men march barefoot!

Soldiers trained to fight using very heavy wooden swords and shields to build their muscles. They practiced techniques like quickly lunging forward to stab with their sword before ducking back behind their shield. They fought against wooden poles, or each other.

It was important to know how to throw a pilum, aim a slingshot, and fire a bow and arrow properly. Soldiers learned how to throw their pila at exactly the same time, creating a deadly shower of spears. A strong soldier could throw his pilum more than 82 feet.

If a soldier made a mistake or didn't do his job properly, he would be punished. Soldiers could be given beatings, fines, and extra jobs, such as scrubbing the latrines (toilets) or extra guard duty. Sometimes they were not given any food rations. If a soldier showed fear during battle or fell asleep while on night watch, punishments were extreme—he could even be beaten or stoned to death!

How did soldiers fight in battle?

The Roman army was well known for its clever tactics during battle. Before a battle began, soldiers were careful to pick the best spot, keeping the sun behind them so that the enemy would be blinded by it. If there was a hill, they tried to make sure they were at the top and the enemy was at the bottom, while the land to the sides was blocked.

When it was time to attack, soldiers made their way to the enemy silently before hurling their spears and charging forward, yelling a scary war cry, with their swords drawn and their shields in front of them.

Soldiers fought shield-to-shield in three battle lines. The youngest stood at the front, using their swords to stab the enemy. The more experienced soldiers stood behind, supporting them with spears and switching with the young soldiers when they got tired. The oldest stood near the back in reserve. Behind them were archers, slingers, and catapultiers.

But Roman soldiers were trained to quickly move into other battle formations, too.

The WEDGE formation was used to crack open enemy lines. Soldiers would form a triangle, like an arrow, with one soldier at the tip. They would then break through the enemy ranks and spread out.

The AQUILIFER was a senior standard bearer who carried the legion's standard (an eagle sculpture on a wooden pole) at the front of the legion. If the eagle standard was lost in battle, it was a disgrace to the legion and the whole army.

The enemies, known by the Romans as "barbarians," weren't just one group of people. There were lots of different European tribes, such as the Goths, Huns, Vandals, and Scots, as well as the Punic, Parthian, and Persian empires.

The SKIRMISH was a widely spaced formation of infantry or cavalry, giving soldiers more room to fight. But it did also allow the enemy more chance to get through, so it was reserved for when the enemy was already in trouble.

The TORTOISE was a strong, tight formation. The soldiers at the front and sides held their shields in front of them so that there were no gaps in between. The soldiers behind held their shields over their heads to form a protective shell roof, which could also be used as a ramp.

The ORB was used as a last resort when the army was outnumbered and losing a battle. Soldiers formed a circle with their shields held in front of them and fought any enemies who came close.

What did cavalry soldiers do?

Cavalry soldiers fought on horseback. They had to be highly skilled horse riders, as well as being very strong and acrobatic so that they could quickly jump on and off their horses and even leave their horses to climb the walls of enemy cities. It took a lot of practice to be able to use their weapons while riding at high speed.

A SPATHA sword was longer than the legionary's gladius so that a cavalry soldier could reach down to the enemy from up on their horse.

A flat, oval-shaped shield was less bulky than the legionary scutum.

The horse's harness and tack were decorated with impressive medallions and metal plates.

Some cavalry soldiers in Africa and Asia even rode camels!

Some cavalrymen were couriers, galloping across the empire's road network to deliver messages, or guards stationed along the highways, looking out for travelers. Some went ahead of the army to gather information on the enemy. Others fought in battle, often brought in toward the end to chase after the fleeing enemies.

To stay on the horse, a cavalry soldier had to use his thighs to grip very tightly on to the four-horned saddle.

The stirrups that horse riders use today hadn't been invented yet, but the cavalrymen did have special spikes on the heels of their shoes called "spurs" to urge the horse forward.

A cavalryman carried several pila, which he threw while charging at the enemy. It took a lot of skill to do this on a galloping horse!

Not only did a cavalry soldier have to spend a lot of time polishing his armor, he also had to groom and feed his horses, as well as keep the saddle, harness, and tack in good condition. For this reason, he was usually paid better than a foot soldier and often brought an enslaved groom along to help him.

What was a siege?

If the enemies were hidden away behind their castle or city walls, the Roman army would plan a siege. This needed plenty of practice and a lot of powerful weapons.

A wobbly ladder could be used to reach the top of an enemy wall, but a more advanced construction was the siege tower. This was a wooden tower that was slightly taller than the fort or city walls, with levels and ladders inside.

Soldiers could push the tower on its wheels toward the wall. Then they could climb to the top and fire their arrows.

A drawbridge at the top of a siege tower could be lowered to let soldiers climb onto the top of the castle walls and then attack from the inside! To stop the tower from being set on fire by the enemy, it could be soaked in water and covered in metal or animal skins.

Sometimes soldiers dug a tunnel underneath the wall of the castle or city, or dug a mine to make the wall collapse.

Soldiers could also batter down doors, walls, or gates at close quarters with a battering ram, which was made of wood and metal.

Soldier Slip-Ups!

Catapults were not very accurate, which meant that boulders could sometimes land in the wrong place, and even injure the Romans themselves!

Attackers sometimes catapulted severed heads, dead bodies, or animal carcasses. This was not only disgusting and scary, but it also helped spread disease within the castle or city.

Defenders sometimes fired back their own artillery, including pots of stinging creepy-crawlies.

ONAGER catapults could fire enormous rocks from a sling. These rocks could weigh up to 175 pounds (about the weight of 12 bowling balls).

Catapults damaged walls to make them ragged and climbable, knocked down towers, set fire to wooden structures, and killed anyone they hit.

A BALLISTA was like a giant crossbow, used to fire bolts or stones at soldiers.

If they didn't win right away, Roman soldiers surrounded the settlement to stop any enemies from escaping. Sieges could continue for days, weeks, or months until the starving enemies surrendered.

What happened if soldiers were injured?

All Roman army camps and forts had a hospital. Treatment was basic compared to hospitals today, but it was much better than any other military medicine in the world at that time.

Roman doctors knew how to clean wounds and stitch them up, set broken bones, and stop infections. If bones were badly broken, the doctor might amputate the damaged limb! The only anesthetics back then were natural ones made from plants and alcohol, and there was no antiseptic so treatment would have been incredibly painful and dangerous.

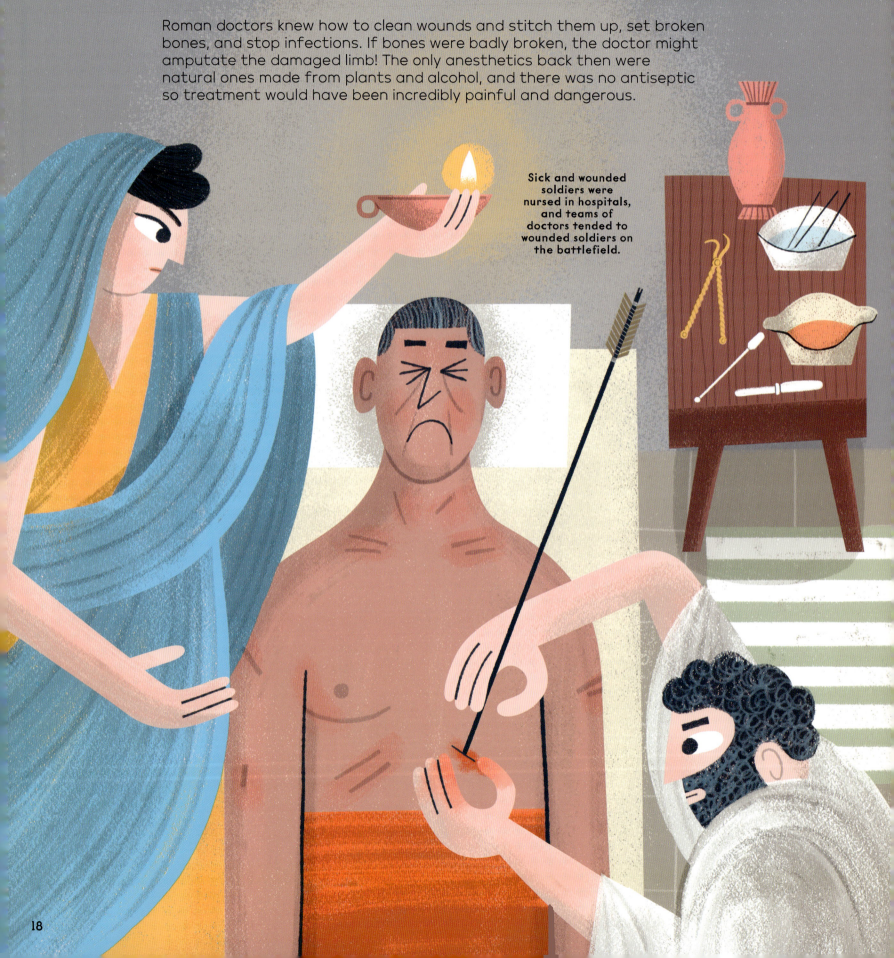

Sick and wounded soldiers were nursed in hospitals, and teams of doctors tended to wounded soldiers on the battlefield.

Even though the Romans didn't know about the tiny cells called bacteria, and how they can cause disease and infection, doctors did know how important it was to keep tools and bandages clean by boiling them in hot water to prevent infections.

If a soldier was so badly injured that they were too weak to fight or developed a disabling condition, they were medically retired.

An army doctor's toolkit:

WINE, VINEGAR, OR OLIVE OIL
To clean wounds

LINEN BANDAGES
To cover wounds

FORCEPS OR TWEEZERS
To remove small pieces of bone or arrowheads

NEEDLE AND THREAD
To stitch up wounds

SCALPEL
To cut through the skin during surgery

BONE SAW
To amputate limbs

SURGICAL CLAMP
To prevent blood loss

ANTISEPTICS
Such as honey and acetum (vinegar), to clean wounds

SPATULA
To spread ointment

HOT WATER
To sterilize (clean) surgical tools and bandages

NATURAL MEDICINE
Such as henbane, opium poppy, and white mandrake root, to help with pain or send a patient to sleep

What was life like in the forts?

Roman soldiers mostly lived inside forts. These were a little bit like Roman cities with a hospital, a bathhouse, workshops, and sometimes even an amphitheater. There was usually a village nearby, where soldiers could go during their time off.

Soldiers could spend years in one fort, so they would get to know the people in the local village well.

Ordinary soldiers slept in buildings called barracks, which were basic, cold, and cramped.

Each contubernium (unit of eight men) had two small rooms. In one, there were bunks to sleep in. In the other, they could keep all their kit and there was a stove for cooking their food.

At mealtimes, soldiers ate meat (usually pork) with fish sauce, bread, or plain biscuits, and then washed it down with beer and wine. They might also have had cabbage, beans, lentils, apples, olives, eggs, beef, lamb, goat, hare, deer, and fresh fish if they were available.

Soldier Slip-Ups!
Sometimes fresh food was difficult to find. A soldier named Terentianus reported that he and many fellow soldiers couldn't work for five days because they had eaten old fish which gave them terrible food poisoning.

The latrine was where soldiers went to the bathroom and shared gossip. Rather than private stalls, there were long wooden benches with holes cut in them for toilet seats. And instead of toilet paper, there were sponges on sticks or balls of moss, which everyone shared!

In their time off from training, soldiers could bathe at the bathhouse. There were cold and warm pools, a sauna, and a steam room. But bathhouses were not just for getting clean—soldiers also went there to keep warm in the central heating, catch up with friends, and play a game of dice.

A centurion had his own house at the end of the barrack block, while higher-ranking officers had large, grand homes. Unlike the lower ranks, centurions and higher officers were allowed to have a wife, children, and servants who lived in their house and moved around the empire with them.

Ordinary Roman soldiers were not allowed to marry, but many of them did have partners or unofficial families in the village nearby.

Where did soldiers live when they were on the move?

When soldiers were on a march, they built camps to live in. These camps had the same layout as a fort, but the soldiers slept in leather tents rather than barracks, and there were no latrines or bathhouses. Soldiers were often much colder and more uncomfortable than usual, and definitely a lot smellier!

Sites would be carefully chosen well in advance on level ground, close to a water source, and ideally on higher ground than the enemy. When the army arrived at the site, they had just a couple of hours to build the camp, since they might move on the next day. Each soldier had a job, from unloading supplies to pitching tents.

It wasn't just soldiers who lived in these camps. Some empresses, women, and children stayed there too, leaving behind the luxuries of their homes to live in the camp alongside the army.

The soldiers who built Hadrian's Wall slept in tents while their barracks were under construction.

The 73-mile-long wall was built during the reign of Emperor Hadrian to mark the border of the Roman Empire in Britannia (the Roman name for the island of Great Britain).

Hadrian's Wall took years to build. Luckily, over time, the soldiers also built forts so they didn't have to spend all that time living in tents. A total of 10,000 soldiers were needed to guard the wall!

What happened when the army won a battle?

When the Romans won a battle, a grand victory parade, known as a "triumph," would be held in the city of Rome—even if the battle had taken place in another country. It was originally a parade for the commander who had won the battle, but over time the emperors began to reserve this grand occasion all for themselves, whether they had led the army directly or not.

The army would march through the streets of Rome, with the emperor riding in a golden horse-drawn chariot, his face painted red to look like Jupiter, the king of the Roman gods.

One servant had the job of standing behind the emperor on his chariot, whispering in his ear to remind him that he was not a god.

Crowds of Romans cheered as the army paraded through the streets—carrying the treasures and riches stolen from the people they had conquered—and jeered at the enemy prisoners chained up.

Senators and other politicians walked at the front of the parade, sharing the glory even if few had been involved in the battle. Behind them, animals were paraded before being sacrificed.

Some victory parades lasted for days, with great banquets, games, and entertainment taking place in the evenings.

Glossary

AMPHITHEATER An open circular or oval building with seats surrounding a central space used as an arena for sporting or dramatic events

ANESTHETIC A medicine that stops you from feeling pain

ANTISEPTIC A substance that stops germs from growing and can be used to clean wounds

AQUILIFER A senior Roman standard bearer who carried the legion's standard (an eagle sculpture on a wooden pole) at the front of the legion

AUXILIARY A soldier in a regiment where they were not required to be a Roman citizen

BALLISTA A weapon similar to a crossbow that could be used to fire bolts or stones

BARBARIAN Anyone that the Romans saw as the enemy

BARRACKS The buildings in a fort where most soldiers lived and slept

BATTERING RAM A large, heavy piece of metal and wood used to force open doors or knock down walls

BRACAE Leggings or pants made of wool

BRITANNIA The Latin name for Great Britain

CALIGAE Sandals worn by Roman soldiers with hobnails in the sole

CAVALRY Soldiers who fought on horseback

CENTURION The commander of a century

CENTURY A group of about 80 men, within a cohort

CINGULUM MILITARE A special soldier's belt with decorated leather straps hanging from it

CITIZEN A person with legal membership rights of a country, either because they inherited them or because they were given, or paid for, legal membership

COHORT A grouping of usually six centuries—about 500 soldiers

CONTUBERNIUM A unit of eight soldiers sharing the same barrack room

EMPEROR A man who rules an empire

FORT A large, rectangular military camp where soldiers lived

GLADIUS A short stabbing sword with a one-and-a-half-foot-long steel blade

GREAVES Armor for the shins

HADRIAN'S WALL A wall linking up forts that was built across northern England by the Romans to control the frontier of Roman Britain

LEGATE The commander of the legion, chosen by the emperor

LEGIONARY A foot soldier who is a citizen of Rome and part of a legion

MANICA A piece of armor to protect the arm

MEDALLION A large medal, worn for decoration

ONAGER A catapult that could fire enormous rocks

OPTIO The centurion's second in command

PILUM A heavy iron spear, like a javelin but weighted and with a sharp point to pierce enemy armor and shields

PRAEFECTUS CASTRORUM A senior soldier, third in charge of the legion

PUGIO A dagger

SCUTUM A long curved shield made of three layers of wood, a thin layer of leather or fabric, and with metal edges

SPATHA A long sword used by the cavalry

STANDARD BEARER A senior soldier who carried a large pole with a badge or flag attached (called a standard), and assisted a centurion

TRIBUNE An officer who worked for the legate and was more senior than a centurion

Index

A
AMPHITHEATER 20, 26
AQUILIFER 12, 26
ARMOR 8–9, 15, 26
AUXILIARIES 4–5, 26

B
BARBARIANS 13, 26
BARRACKS 20–23, 26
BATHHOUSES 20–22
BATTLE 4, 6–14, 18, 24–25
BOW AND ARROW 11
BRITANNIA 23

C
CAMPS 7, 9, 17–18, 22–23, 26
CATAPULT 12, 17, 26
CAVALRY 13–15, 26
CENTURION 6, 21, 26
CENTURY 6, 21, 26
CLOTHING 8–9
COHORT 6, 26
CONTUBERNIUM 6, 20, 26

D
DOCTORS 18–19

E
EMPEROR 7, 10, 23–24, 26
EMPIRE 4, 13–14, 21, 23, 26

F
FAMILIES 21
FIGHTING 7, 9, 11–13, 19
FOOD 5, 10–11, 20
FORTS 9, 16, 18, 20–23, 26

G
GLADIUS 9, 14, 26

H
HADRIAN'S WALL 23
HORSES 13–15, 24, 26
HOSPITAL 18–20

I
INJURY 14, 17–19

J
JAVELIN 12, 15, 26

L
LATRINES 11, 21–23
LEGATE 7, 26
LEGION 6–7, 12, 26
LEGIONARIES 4, 6

M
MARCHING 6, 10, 22, 24
MEDICINE 18–19

O
OPTIO 6, 26
ORB 13

P
PILUM 9, 11, 26
PRAEFECTUS CASTRORUM 7, 26
PUGIO 9, 26
PUNISHMENT 6, 11

R
REWARDS 5

S
SCUTUM 9, 14, 26
SHIELD 9–14, 26
SIEGE 16–17
SKIRMISH 13
SLINGSHOT 11
SPATHA 14, 26
STANDARD BEARER 6, 12, 26
SWORD 8–9, 11–12, 14, 26

T
TACTICS 4, 12, 16
TORTOISE 13
TRAINING 6, 10–13, 21
TRIBUNE 7, 26
TRIUMPH 24–25

U
UNIFORM 8–9

V
VICTORY PARADE 24–25

W
WEAPONS 8–16
WEDGE 12